Between the writer and the reader is an inevitable chasm.

On one side the writer crafts from a repertoire of vocabulary the sentences to convey a reflection, an emotion an observation, the essence of an experience.

Tthe reader seeks to extract from the words on the page what that infusion of personality, culture and experience has led to.

To the sender and receiver a poem can deliver the enjoyment and gladness of a craft well executed, a thought worth knowing and a sentiment exchanged.

Each delves into a quantum of meaning, a concoction of wordage in the format of poesy as understood in this age.

The divide is stretched further by the singularity of our separate mental islands of individuality, by culture and perspective.

That the chasm is bridged so often is a wonder of humanity.

From my side of the abyss can I say that these poems give me joy when I read them and that I had pleasure in the writing of them.

They are the lint of the nap of a life.

I hope you enjoy them and they give you pleasure and that you see a sliver of the world that I saw when I was in it.

Published by

Daniel McCaffrey
P O Box 6280
Wellington 6141
New Zealand

ISBN 978-0-9876530-0-0

Daniel McCaffrey

mccaffrey.daniel@gmail.com

Contents

8	....	For times to come
11	....	The Alone crowd
12	....	The Policy
15	....	Such riches in a book.
16	....	Walking
17	....	A Blessed Land
18	....	The Recipe
22	....	What is
31	....	Wellington
33	....	The Music
35	....	The Wren
36	....	The Hedge at Clonmel
38	....	A Founder of the State
40	....	Over There
42	....	Melike the Cat
44	....	Adam
47	....	Mare Nostrum
49	....	Le Fly
51	....	Le Fly - The Roomey
52	....	Le Fly III - Trouble
54	....	The Coast Road
56	....	The Cote de Azur
57	....	In Cannes
59	....	Air New Zealand Flight 035
60	....	A Day Came
61	....	Flutter by Butterfly
52	....	They love you Still
60	....	Caroline's Prayer

Contents

65	....	God and the Ants
67	....	The Small Dinosaurs
68	....	The Tide Turns
69	....	The Dark Awaits
70	....	I had a bath Today
72	....	A Child
74	....	Three Gifts
75	....	Mars and the Non criminals
77	....	To be Irish
78	....	Running from Goma
79	....	I Feel Death
80	....	The Artist
82	....	Land, Sea and Air
84	....	The Wave
86	....	For Oleg
88	....	Icons
89	....	Looking for God
91	....	Courage
92	....	Donagh Cross
93	....	Cara
95	....	The Quad
96	....	Without you
98	....	Nua.ie
99	....	Belair
100	....	Adelaide - Summer
101	....	Adelaide - Birds
102	....	Adelaide – Autumn Leaves

Contents

103 .... Rory and the Ants

105 .... Details

106 .... In the English Channel

107 .... Squiggles

108 .... Coming to the PSA Council

109 .... Franklin Road

110 .... Adams Cats

111 .... Spring 1984

112 .... Adam's Kittens

113 .... Muldoon

114 .... For Donal

115 .... At 97

116 .... On the Train to Oxford

117 .... Harry and Cecilia

118 .... The Stranger

119 .... Graffiti

120 .... Big Sur

121 .... Sea Island Vancouver

122 .... The Old Men

123 .... Wet Steers

124 .... On Lines of Faulkner

125 .... Notes on poems

It was an idea so dangerous
that he was afraid to let it out of the house.
So he locked it away in a room in his head
and hoped it would go away.
It didn't.
He visited it occasionally
and observed how it had grown
and acquired nuances and implications.

He was afraid that
when he left the house himself
He would blurt it out over lunch
or after a drink in the pub.

It was a dangerous idea no doubt of it.
Maybe it didn't need him to voice it anyway.
Perhaps it was just an accident
that it germinated in his head first.
In time more people
would stumble upon the notion.
And then it could spread on its own,
like a quantum virus.

Galloping from loose tongue to loose tongue
Morph, manipulate and change how people
behaved.

It could fall into the hands of fanatics and zealots.
That had happened before to alluring ideas.
Worse it might fall into the hands of governments
With the power and money to implement it.

There had been so many memes through history,
notions ideological beliefs
that had destroyed many good lives
and mind you some that had brought great good.

When everyone had the idea he thought
Then they would have to take collective
responsibility for its terrible portends.
The best thing might be done not the worst.
He would be off the hook.

So would it be better to wait
and to read all about it in the newspapers,
one day.

Or would that be cowardly.
Better to do the decent thing.
Be brave.
Go into that room in his head
and sit down with the idea
while it was getting on its feet
and talk it over.

To use the faculties of his mind
to explore the possible conjugations
and try hard to work out a solution.

A way forward through the dangers and horrors.
Perhaps when that was done
he could take the idea out in the daylight
And introduce it to the world,
a bright new notion.

Safe
with its positive aspects accentuated
and its evil potential defanged.

He was tempted to found a society
an association for the destruction
and refutation
and disproval
of dangerous notions.

And maybe open a foster home for good ideas
that had been ill treated when they were young
and growing.

The world so desperately need new good ideas.
And so urgently needed to discard the vile ones.

If you lean over I could whisper it to you
He said.

Wellington 2015

The Alone Crowd

We are the alone crowd
Here, all together
On a Sunday afternoon
All alone, together
At the library

For whatever reason this is our refuge
Where being alone is ok
Escapees from life's disasters
That deserved or otherwise left us here
alone together

It's a good collective.
All only on their own.
and the rules help.
No talking is allowed.

But we don't go home alone
We take home old and new friends
in the pages and videos
Bringing .into our alone lives
people who live dramatically crowded lives.
Lives we can only imagine.

Later on alone - at home
these people will talk to us
In the small black letters sprinkled in words on
white paper, talking quickly page by page.

We are the alone crowd
And in the library
On Sunday afternoons
We stick together
Keeping ourselves to ourselves
Alone - apart - together - Alone

Wellington Library Sunday Afternoon April 2015

The Policy

I should tell you
how the phrases were framed
and placed like machine guns
snug and tight
in long tin boxes.
Fitting in the wooden slots provided.
with each word in the magazines
exact and explicit
setting out measured,
made and determined, your life to be.

May I say the discussion at conferences
where we heard the policy delineated,
notched in bullet points on whiteboards
went as well as expected.

Negotiations were held
with the interested parties.
The lobbyists were lunched.
It was signed off by the civil servants
advised upon by the academics
All the stake holder were squared away
everyone consulted.
Well, except you.

So this straight jacket
this policy framework
is where you will live your life.

Oh I know they never asked you.
You attended no meeting.
You didn't know them
and they never knew you
or anybody like you.

You're an average.
A statistic.
A theoretical construct.
The words and numbers
made their transition
from the abstract theory
matters set out in the policy submissions
To the writing of the proposal
To the policy
Without any knowledge of you
your life, your affairs.

Its now written, the policy.
Pages of prescription in bright shiny folders
ready for execution
Signed off.
To be made into the majesty of law.

Yes I know
you won't be at the select committee.
Nobody like you ever is.
There will be new clauses.
Supplementary Order Papers.
The bill will be argued
at the committee stages
in your house of representatives.
But then your not represented by anybody.

And after the governor general
has signed the bill
it will be the law.

And directives will flow from the Minister
and guidelines will be issued
by the department.

And finally the pamphlet will arrive
maybe, maybe not
in your letter box.

Be sure you do as you are told
You could lose the benefit if you don't.
Life could get unpleasant.

And do report any change in circumstances
to the department.
We may not have told you
but you certainly must tell us.
The policy takes into account
any change in circumstances.
As it should
As it should.

Please complete the attached form

Wellington March 2015

Such riches in a book.

It is a respect for words
in a tribute paid by a city to itself.
Reflecting the fact that the poets
in the first instance
felt moved enough by the city
to gift it with the words and sentiments
it evoked from them.

So they bequeathed to Dublin
a legacy of the view of itself
that became what it was and is
as much as the roads
and buildings and stones and monuments.

A notion of the town which became riven
in the souls of the people of the city.

And all together
the people of the past and present
and the poets of the present and past
and the writers of songs
and the singers of them
and the crafters of the books
and the readers of them

they made a Dublin that was transportable.
A city in the mind
that could be carried away in the head
and felt and seen in any place and time.

"If you go" Dadalus Press City of Dublin.
http://www.dublinonecityonebook.ie /node/362
Wellington April 2 2014

Walking

I walk through my memories
along Swanson Road.

Past a school I legalised
when I was a legal clerk.
Pass by a street named after Frank Evans
a man about whom I wrote a play.

And walk into a constituency
in which I stood for parliament.

A truck goes by with a shipping container
from Hamburg Sud.
I worked for them as a boy
briefly at sea.

Is it that I have done so much
or that the web of memory is
peeping through a very present minute.

Henderson 2011

Beyond Here

You are the lands rim, the western edge
furrowed into the stormed Atlantic.

It is your wild coast
that brings to an end.
The finality of all the lands that stretch
back to Kamchatcka

From here - facing to the set sun
the waves toss row on row to America

All the counties draped along these shores
Donegal Sligo Leitrim Mayo Galway
Clare Limerick Kerry and Cork
are stamped with wildness
the glint of rock and the heft of mountains
and glistened sea spray
furling along the bronzy strands.

The butter cupped fields
blessed continual with the sacredness of rain
once a greenness blurred in tears
glimpsed across the ship rail
by your leaving children.

Now framed far and small
in an aircraft window
as the plane arcs up to 40,000 feet

A small glimpse hauntingly remembered
till our return.

May 2014 Wellington

A Blessed Land

The love of God for Ireland
lies plain before your gaze
at the foot of Slievenamon.

It whispers in the
windy leafy lanes
threaded among fields
coaxed by hedges.

It spreads like ivy under
chestnut trees.
Flares white along the roads
in hawthorn blossomed spring
sleeps peaceful in ruined monasteries

The love of God
for this blessed island
gleams in the moonlight
shines like the sun
over the honey meadows
around Cluin Meal.

Wellington 2014

The Recipe

It was there in plain words
written out with a pencil.
Agnes's Wheaten bread.
And they all had it, the recipe.
Cath Doran, Mrs Coll and Nell Delaney.
But the words weren't enough .

It said about a cup or so,
so being maybe more than that
or it could be less, of sour milk.
The bottle sitting in the window ledge for
days.
And God help any stranger washing the
dishes
who thought they were doing Ma a favour
by throwing out the sour milk
and washing the bottles.

Bread production would stop for days while
their mental capacities
were called in question.

How sour, well sour, not rotten,
or gone to the green water.
The words didn't capture that.

And the half white flour
and the half wheaten meal
Well that was plain enough,
but there was the smidgen of a room for
doubt even there.

And how much, a couple of cups, but what
size, Crown Lynn?

She never used cups to measure anything,
what was wrong with handfuls?

Hands were always at hand were they not.
And a pinch of salt, not over a teaspoon.
That was all.

Could there be a simpler recipe?

They never got it right.
Their's always turned out brown.
You would eat it as politeness dictated
and you had to say it was as good as Ag's.
But it never was.

It wasn't green and soft.
It was brown and hard.
And again politeness meant
though they knew it wasn't
anywhere near the bread that Agnes made.
They would say they were pleased
you had said so.

Even as they knew as you did
that it wasn't.
It must have been the mixing, the kneading,
the length of time it was in her hands
and whatever knack she had of doing it that
made it soft and green.
Maybe you needed her size of hands
Or was it you kneaded it less?

Could it be she had it in a slow oven,
gently rising it
Not a word was said about temperature

Was that Ag's secret?
Its possible they roasted it hard and fast and
Made it stiff and brown.

She was always pleased politely and without
saying a hard word, sympathetic even
when she heard
they had no success making it.

But there was no doubt
Only she could do it.
Get it so that it was soft sweet and sharpish
tangy green with the crisp crust
to be buttered on its own
Or fried in butter and bacon with eggs
and black pudding and sausages and a chop
An essential portion of the Ulster fry.

But it was hers and when she went it went
with her.
And no matter if you scoured the shops from
Lisnaskea to Larne
You could never buy wheaten bread like Ag's
and try as anyone might or could
will, anyone read the recipe
simple as it is
and
make a loaf of wheaten bread like Ag.

Wellington January 2 2015

What is

Is

has an "isness"
an essentiality
a presence.

Which allows a conscious entity
A sentient being
Like a human being
To come along
take what is

And
extrapolate it
Describe it
attribute it
Construct stories,
text about what is

Recognise what is
Paint what is
Speak of what is
Represent what is

Humans
can get what is
and have it
Illuminated
Made into metaphor
Wordified
Allegorised
Extrapolated

They can roll what is
through the mind
turn it over in words
on the tongue.

An enterprising human being
may seize the billion
trillion trillion
constituent elements
the quintessential essence
of what is.

And
name the parts
make them congruent
title them
number them
mathematise them
adumbrate them
encapsulate them
label them.

For humans the totality of is
Can be theorised with science
hypothesised, conjugated and Inferred.

Human beings
may flirt with
the reality
the truth
the essence
of what is

may even
from the assumptions
and wispy nuances of

that they think what is
is
have the bravado of mind
to predict
what will be
what might be.

By the effort of imagination
in Myth, Religion Fiction
say
What is is

They can declare
without a ounce of reality
from an imagined imagery
the thinkness of thought
in the minds dreamy haze.
with an ideas room of mirrors
of an imagined what is
bring a granite fastness
more real than the is of
what is.
(or so they think)

Peoples from the hands creation
out of the minds eye
construct the tools of cinema
television, the plays stage
the Internet.

The songs emanation
can enswathe
a gloriously conceited
concoction
a fabricated conception
of a what is
that might be

but maybe is not
what is.

Or a gloriously entertaining
What is not

What is difficult
if not impossible is
for a many
to agreed on
what is.

To reach an agreement
by the who are
as to who is we
and out conclusions
on the what is.

What if
The assemblage of the
who are
cannot agree on the
what is?

True there may be yes
exchanged views
Notions
Ideas
Statements
Opinions
Outlines
On what is

As interpreted
Understood
Discussed agreed
Voted on

Accepted as gospel
Finally stipulated
With absolute certainty
by the who are.

Yet so hard a thing is it
for the who are to concur
that agreement can vanish in a moment

What is churlishly does not do
what was assumed
by the who are
and concurrance
vanishes into
notness.

Alas not even the what was
can be considered safe
as agreed
certain
definitely the
touchstone of what was.

There are as many interpretations
multiplied
by the number of beings
and adding twenty for good measure
on what was is
that casts a multitude of doubt
on what we agreed about what is
once was.

And as for the what will be.

Well
most of the we s

don't even bother to consider
where what will be
is to start from.

The beginning point
the Dublin road
start of the matter.

There is little wonder then
on the disagreement
of where to
to the what will be
by the who is we.
in the what is

Its all a hologram of conjecture
A notion
An ideology
A view.

Meanwhile
I suspect that what is
all the immensity
carries on being What is
Undisturbed by the cogitations.

After all
If the notions, assumptions conjectures,
impressions, wordifications
don't escape from the paper.

Leap from the picture frame
or pass beyond words on the lips
of the who
and the who is we s.

If they remain in the discussion halls
and the libraries.
There is little to worry about

They will remain words lightly spoken
What is to be will not be
but stay vicarious what is's

What is's that we thought happened
But did not
stay just abstract conclusions of
academia
notions that never grasped what is

There is a danger though
that mistaken notions
of what is
what was
and what may be.

Run rampant through the heads of politicians
and bureaucrats
soaking up trillions of taxpayers dollars.

Its then
they become the stuff of hideous nightmares
Leading to poverty and despair.

No
It's only when lunatically unreal phantomisms
of the self appointed elite
have got their hands on the power to tax
to wield the power of the state
and the police and the army
are marched out on a reality thwarting
what is.

When the bars of cells are ready
for the taxpayers unable to flee
from a what will be lunacy of notions
Galaxies in distance from what is
That the trouble starts.
Keep it small I say
very small.
Tiny steps at a time.
Let the who is we
be small

let the what is to be
be well inspected
before
it is turned in to disastrous phantasms '
Of waste and destruction by the
Those who are not we
Befouling the what is
Into the what will be

Best to
Grope to the who is we
A step at a time
Talking often together

So we concur on the what is
very precisely
As much as we can
Before any big plans for the what will be
Are laid in place.

Gather as many facts as we can
and agree on them
before launching opinions

Wellington

I shall remember this city as a waltz
A dance of winds
with a huntaway dog
mustering tumults of clouds
across the harbour sky
to the north
then
to the south.

In the morning the sun
coming up over the Orongorongos
faltering, high and waiting.
First shining in the windows of the Hutt
then rolling out a shimmered path
in the water from Petone.

Night and the orange stick men
of the streets lights
ams outstretched
march up the Wainuiomata road.

Richard
striding determined down the road
from up near Kaiwharawhara
Looking in every rubbish bin
all the way to Cambridge Terrace.
then going home
if home he has.

I will always bring to mind
the houses hung like paintings
impossibly perched
on the green walled hills.
The flowers on Onslow road.

The sparrows by the bus stop
at Courtney place
Hustling the café crowds
for one tiny morsel of a meal.

The pirouetting crowds in Cuba Mall.
The railway station trains
Gliding in to the platforms
in stately quadrills
at the end of the golden mile.

I shall remember this city as a dance.

Khandallah February 2014

The Music

I miss the music.
The lilt and heft of it.
The passion and suasion
roiling out of time immemorial.

The dreaminess of a slow air
drifting magic across a room
like a wafting feather.

The brash enthusiastic clatter of a jig.
A dancers feet hitting every note
rattling the floor
following the weaving beat
waiting for the bar.

Pipes cleaving through chords
old beyond knowing.

An accordion
chasing the concertina
and the whistle
like a sparkling piccolo
leading the melodion
the flute and fiddle
in a hornpipe
wildness in every haunting step.

And a singer
caressing the cadence of every word.
Breathe wrapping the tongue
to the perfection of the soul.
The harmonies chalicing
the grace of people
drawing the listeners into the tale.

In homage to the framers of the tune
and the storied spirit
of now
and long ago.

I love the bands,
their messaged eyes
and nods to each other.
Entwining minds
into flying hands
and placed fingers
and tapping feet.

The songs evoking past
and future
retelling the secrets
of the hearts dreams.

The joy and smiling
young old
lost
in melody.

Wellington St Patricks Day 2014

The Wren

Hopping turning jerking.

A hopesy bouncy cheerfulness.

You are the essence of optimism.

Bobbing possibilities
in every fibre of your tiny frame
exuding hope and promise.

An impudent tail
angular impossibly
propped up
right angled
behind that small small body.

You are always
a joy.

Clonmel 2013

The Hedge at Clonmel

The sun glittering in shaded blinking
as the wind fluttered leaves
flicker the glitters of the light
in through the stems and
woodness of the fronds.

On one side
the lane
on the other
the grass and flowers of the meadow.

In behind the secrecy of the shimmered
greenness of the leaves
wrens, red breasts and tits.
Safe secure
in warm moss lined nests.

Small hearted life
chirping the coming
of a new half feathered generation.

A hopeful clutch of fledglings
in the still drawing line
of the hundreds and thousands
who have gone before them
progenitors of who will follow
in this twigness of the world.

Soon brave for
scared timid
then braver forays
out from the leafy long rowed castle
of their half lit domain.

To sweep and dart
quick and wheeling
into the mothy swathes of
the evening.

Night falling
the waning of the dimming light
slowly fading into the silent darkness.

The dawn rising cautious and slow
fingering the hedgy edges
wafting the warming rays
in through the foliage.

And from branch and twig
the songs of the tiny souls
singing out their hearts
to God and all mankind.
A new day born,
a term of hours,
free and glad.

Clonmel, County Tipperary

A Founder of the State.

Does it count
that he strove for it's freedom.
Made a life of it
when left in the balance
was a pinch faced misery.

Schemed and toiled
in incessant war
first with the enemy
then with his own.

A constant and continual
barrage of dispute
that became a badge of the state
alway for parting and dividing
separating and hating.

Are we to wonder
that from his smile less eyes
came the mirthless
calvinistic joyless decades
overlaid
with the drear shadow of Maynooth.

The stiff armless dancing.
The blind obedience
to church and clergy.

Turning well meant intentions
to poor eventuations.

The stifling of infant prosperity.

What we do know
is that through it all
the songs gushed out.

The music lived always
and the spirit of the people
held its ground.

Hope then
that the love of joy and their God
has finally wrested the country
and its
culture
from his dark cold embrace.

Clonmel, Co Tipperary, August 2013

Over There 1955.

Over there
when we crossed the border
to go to mass in Clones
the road signs
came in a strange unknown language.

The monuments were
to the glorious heroes of 1916.

And the telephone boxes were green
with the word telephone
obviously misspelt.

Back there
in the place
where we had come from
near Newtonbutler.
The statues of the tin hatted soldiers
were to the slain on the Somme.

And the telephone boxes
as every one knows
all over the world,
were like the one we knew
at granny McGinnity's shop
in Essnadarragh
were red
as they should be.

Coming home to Cara,
back from mass.
We felt the flinty cold demeanour
of the B specials
as they searched the car for butter.

They let us know
in brisk orderly terms
that we were not welcomed back
to where we had come from
and been
for thousands of years.

Neither of the peoples of these countries
owned up to us.

Or paid our views and interests any respect
as they fought quarrels of their own
over and around us.

Destroying our way of earning a living
in the murder and muddle of the border
campaign.

So
one March day

We left.

Clonmel 2013

Melikie the cat

Melikie looks from the fourth floor balcony
of the apartment of Jose in Salamanca.

And sees the cathedral towers
with the storks standing over their nests.

He sees the trees and the people passing
to and fro
on the Calle Santa Clara.

Doves and pigeons
cruise past in aerial procession
before his eyes.
on the balcony
of the apartment of Jose
in Salamanca.

He flicks his tail and listens
to the chattering song of the small birds.
Out and before him is a world
he has never experienced.

He walks and stalks
back through the apartment
to find a bottle top
or some strange thing
to hunt
and chase
and capture.

The people in the apartments
sometimes go to the banks of the Tormes
to see the birds
and watch the wind
move the trees
and hear the river
cascade in noisy humour
over the weir.

They live
enmeshed in their screens
in their high lofts.

In the world of books
and writings
sitting with Melikie
watching a universe
of looks and feels
they can scarcely imagine.

Somewhere
out there
beyond the balcony
of the apartment of Jose
in the city
of Salamanca.

Salamanca 2013

Adam

Youth are blessed
with a profundity of ignorance.
They know little of the past
and the present
is a conjugation of surprise.

They are to be taught,
as they look at the world
with their new eyes,
the truths and lies
of how
what is
has come to pass
and
what will be
is theirs to make.

For the future is unquestionable theirs.
In time
the current makers of the myths
and truths
and the reality
of the world they live in
will die
and pass into the recording of history.

They are blessed with curiosity
and lofty presumptions
and will in time
choose between the truths,
wisdoms and lies of the world
that has been placed at their feet.

They will
and must
make judgements
from their learning
in books and lecture halls.

They have yet to learn
the responsibility
of making a decision
on uncertain knowledge
amid the tirades of people
of all notions
narrowing
the paths of possibility.

What if they could stand
on the bridge facing Lars Porcenna
or sit in the Hall of mirrors in Versailles
and make that decision.

Or stand before the seat of Pilate
And shout
Jesus.
When all about them
their friends and fellow citizens
demand that Barrabas
the murderer
should live
and
Christ
should die.

The banquet of possibilities
a surfeit of choice
is always present

Concer
esperanza,
filimente.

The world
has yet
to be.

Salamanca May 2013

Mare Nostrum

The contrails rise
from the southern rim of the horizon
and move up the centre of the sky.

Planes and seated passengers
five miles high
crossing this sea
from Africa.

This is mare nostrum,
Our Sea.
From its rims edges
came the Phoenicians.
At its shores
stood Pharaohs and Emperors.

Across its waters
blew ideas and philosophies.
Notions of the Phonecians, Carthaginians
Greeks, Jews, Romans and Islam.

Across these hills behind me
came Hannibal
marching determinedly to Cannae.
Strode Marius to meet the Cimbri.

In this place and on this shore
the Ligurians
watched the ships of Caesar
come to conquer Gaul.

On that small island there
St Patrick made ready
to preach to the Irish.

Into this sea pours the Nile
the Rhone, Po and the Ebor
and from the Bosphorus
flow the Dnieper and the Don.

The blue wavelets wash
their mingled waters
from Cadiz to Alexander
from Split to Algiers.

If there is a Europe
this is its watery cradle.

The beginning point
of its seminal essence.

Around its shores are the people
who came so far
and on its rim
have so much further to go.

Cannes 2013

Le Fly

Theres a fly
in the middle of the room
in the middle of the air
going back and forth
side to side
fro and back.

Occasionally
changing altitude
for a bit of variety I suppose.

He's been at it for hours.
Doesn't seem to get tired.

He's a French fly
naturally,
this being France.

And a house fly to boot
this being a house.

(You can't say an apartment fly can you)

So he's a mouche maison
or should that be
mouche le maison
or maison de mouche.

No matter.

Of course
he is not a low rent
house fly.

This is after all
is the Cote de Azur
te Riviera no less.

So he's a maison mouche au cote de Azur
from the Riviera.
Classy sort of a guy really.

If you put it like that.

Cannes April 2013

Le fly II - The roomy

He's got tired now
and is resting behind the curtain.
He probably thinks
I can't see him.
But its a white curtain
and he stands out
as he does
like a fly on white paper.

He probably thinks
he can move in
eat the sugar I spill
and hover round my smelly socks.

Make out to the other flies
in the foyer
that he's my flat mate
my roomy
my house guest.

Cheeky bugger
Mr. Mouche.

Cannes April 2013

Le Fly III - Trouble

Flipping heck
now there's two of them

Swirling round the room
tangling
tircling circling.
What's going on?

They are doing some sort of aerial tango
A dans la mouche
Wanton eroticism
in front of my eyes.

Or has one of his seedy mates
come over from Marseille?
And this is some version
of mid air fight club
for flies?

He's got a nerve inviting his mates in.

No hang on a minute.
They are doing a copycat version
of the space shuttle on the top of a 747.

So how's he hanging on?
This is taking a great deal of coordination.
No hang on.

Yeah
that might explain it.
We can drop the two blokes
and the fight theory.

He's invited some floozy in.
Maybe a moocher from Menton
or a scrubber from San Tropez.

If he was any bigger
I'd grab him by the collar
and say
"Listen Mouche."

Too late for that.

Should have hauled him
and his wanton ways
in yesterday.

There goes the neighbourhood.
There's going to be tiny little fly nappies
drying on the balcony
any time soon.

Hundreds of them.

Cannes 2013

The Coast Road

I feel a need to go up that coast again
Begin at Santa Barbara and go up number 1.
Past San Simeon to camp again at Big Sur

Spend some days behind Carmel
feel warm in Salinas and San Louis Obispo

Check if Rod McKuen is still around

Stand on the corner of Haight
sit in the panhandle
and then cross Stanyan Street
walk through the park
where Emmett and the diggers
fed the people.
Chat to the squirrels again.

I want to walk Muir woods
climb Mount Tamalpais
eat in Sausalito
and swim at Russian River.

And after that pass through the Wolf lair
Up the valley to Mendicino County

Drive through Eureka in the fog,
and wander along Coos bay
Light a fire from the drift wood at Astoria

Live again on Sea Island
cook porridge on a primus on Spanish Banks
remember nights in Kitsilano
with mosquitos and Gary.

Camp once more in Horseshoe bay
and talk to the chipmunks.
Bring to back mind their hilarious screechy
battles through the ashes of our campfire.

I thought I seen his work
along this coast in 67
or met some friends of his at least.

Oh I know he loves the world
and all the parts of it
he's made

But I am sure he has his favourite bits
As I do mine.

Cannes April 2013

52

Cote de Azur

The sunlight drenched the streets here today
The brightling light
swathing the buildings in a honeyed
warming glow.

The sky was blue azur
and the mildest wind
ruffled the palm trees.

The Doves kissed each other
on the rail of my balcony

Cote de Azur April 2013

In Cannes

There is a great train of clouds today
marching its way
across the south of the sky.

And underneath it
a soft wind blows
across the blue sea
from Africa.

It rained all day yesterday.
A windless falling rain
that covered all
the buildings
and roads
in a gleaming shiny wetness.

Its snowing.
In the first week of April
it is snowing
all over northern Europe.

From Cushendal to Cracow
In the Alps
and all the way across Croatia
to Romania
and Russia.

The birds
are turning back from Germany
and the spring buds of Bretony
are glaced with snowflakes.

But its warm here
and the mimosa has
blossomed at Mougins.

I seen a red bee
in among the ivy there.

The terracotta roofs
sit snugly into the hill sides.
The oak tree's buds
are ready.

Spring will come.
It always has.
Better late
than never.

Cannes April 2013

Air New Zealand Flight 035

Under this fluffy whiteness over China
lies the Pearl River basin.

Peeps of roads link square housed villages
their shelves of fields clinging to the mountain's
edge.

Suddenly
I am in the northern half of the world.
Now to me as long ago the sun shines
from the southern part of the sky.

As we fly west this morning
it scampers behind us bringing
perpetual daylight.

Liuzhou is under a white pillow case.
The terrible Talimakan and
the edges of Tibet are to the south.
Dushambe Amalty Karganda Furze Urumchi.
Names I have fondled in my mind for years.

Roads streak out across the brown baked
tableau from nowhere to nowhere.
The shrunken Aral Sea then Astrakhan.

Then the white whiteness
of continually white snow
with small black lakes
beads of cold frozen intensity,
that forge the marrow of the Russian soul.

February 26 2013

A day came

This day
came
without any purpose
attached to it.
No label affixed
as to what could be done with it.

No intent was spelled out.

No tasks were attached.

A day
where all consequences
could be unintended.

All actions could be of no particular utility.

A day for the idle spending off.

Redhill Surrey Monday 18 March 2013

Flutter by butterfly

A nonchalant butterfly
without plan
or seeming purpose
flew down Courtney place today.

Among the
pigeons
and people
and sparrows.

Insouciant
and
unconcerned.

It's good to see nonchalance at work.

Wellington February 2013

They love you still

Ah Rabbie man
They've done you proud.
Sitting gowned
a look of whimsy on your face
as you survey this town.

Your breeches tight,
gazing over lawns and buses
and the lovely bonnie lassies.
Fair Mary's word below your feet
and Baxter's plaque behind you.

You would have loved James K.
A man like you in love with words and drink
a Dunedin man
fit well to be your ilk.

They could have placed a prelate here
John Knox or such.
A braw and stern reminder of their
faith and plans
for their new town.

But no
these grave men of the Kirk
they placed a poet here.

A man of roving eye
who loved the girls
and drink for bye.

You and they
'Gave each their promise true'
'Gave you their promise true.'
'Till all the seas gang dry.'
They knew
long after buildings fall
and sermons pass away
the words of poets ring
and that the words of Robbie Burns
will last past ould Lang Syne.

And so it is on every 25th of January
they do remember you.
With fondness in their hearts
and pride in this fine city.

You and they
'Gave each their promise true'
'Gave you their promise true'
'Till all the seas gang dry.'

Ah Rabbie man they love you still.

Dunedin January 2012

A Prayer for Caroline

Thank you lord.

For the twenty six.
For their pliance
and their placing.

With spaces held for meaning
in between the long and short
and grave and joyous
mixture of them.

Scanned out in lines
please God,
page upon page of them
that come from spirits guiding.

Thank you lord
for the twenty four.
Each measure of the minutes,
precious,
laden with the breath of possibility.

Time upon time of them,
moon and sun of them.

Thank you.

Glenelg July 2012

God and the Ants.

God must have had bugger all to do
one wet Sunday afternoon
when he created
two thousand species of Ants
for Australia.

Maybe
he didn't spend a whole afternoon
thinking out
the eensey weensy differences
in their design.

Maybe
it took the smallest fraction
of a millisecond
for the Divine mind
to conjure not one
or ten or even a hundred species
but two thousand
give or take one or two
of the little legged fellows.

And if your going to fill some place
with that many kinds of Ants.
Billions of them
why not Australia.
Its big enough.

If for instance
he had stuck them in Iceland
they would be all on top of each other
tucked up in overcoats and
complaining about the cold.

But still
you wonder.

Two thousand
different
distinct kinds
of the busy little
persons?

He must like them.

I wonder
if he has given them
much thought since.
Or they him?

Parklands Adelaide October 2012

The Small Dinosaurs

The small dinosaurs
fluttered down here today
and cleaned the footpath
outside the shops
of every crumb and speck.

On their spindly legs they hopped
eyes scanning, pecking every scrap
with their small beaks.
Clasping every minute morsel
sharp and sure.

When I was young I was told
that you had died out
60 million years ago.

Yet here you are.
Chirpy feathered flotsam.
Living on crumbs from
someone else's table.

It was clever of you.
Learning to fly, and sing.
You learnt
to sing.

Glenelg   Adelaide 2011

The Tide Turns

First, the aft end
of the boats lifts.

But it is quite some time
before the mid-ship even moves.

As the point
mid way between the stern and bow lifts
the bow raises it's prow
and the whole boat lifts.
It lifts only when the tide is nearly in.

Now,
and only now
can the boat swing around.

Swing the bow around
to the running tide
turning the whole boat
on the foaming tide
so that
the boat can
set out
to the open sea.

Beethoven House January 2012

The Dark Waits,

The Dark waits
with no assumptions.
Like a black linen sheet.
Unmarked.
It has no demands,
merely an invitation
to bargain
to make an offer.

Make an offer
to the light.
An offering
to spirits
who wish to join the dance
of souls and song.

And in the light
in the clear strong light

rejoice
at the coming day.

Written on a Lan Chile Jet   - Sydney Auckland

I had a Bath Today

I had a bath today.
A long luxurious watery bath in heat and
wetness.
That was easier said than done.
So much is said easily
and never done.

Someone broke the old one
so I had to suddenly one morning find a bath
but as someone spoke to another
and I spoke to someone else
I had a bath within the hour.

So I carried it home
with my trusty yellow trolley
and hauled it up the stairs
and tore out the old one
and then built the cradle for the new one.

And fitted and sawed and filed and filled
and was taken to the cleaners by bandits
charging $27 for a tube of filler
and a man from Belfast
taking $2 out of my hand
for a useless drain pipe
and forays to Grey Lynn and Henderson
to buy the exactly right drain pipe.

And so I had a bath today.
As Pisces peeps into the year
and so much has to be done.

I lay in the warm soft lapping water
 as it seeped and soothed
its way into every crevice and pore in my body.

It's different from a shower
a brief dampy hasty wash.

A bath wafts your weight away
 and floats your soul in heated bliss.

Awareness as your neck and toes
And armpits and all the bobbly bits
take the searing wakening.

It seemed like the Baths of Caracalla
where friends seep drowsy
all equal stripped of garb and grandiosity
and say those things that can't be said in
showers, chairs and moments in the elevator.

Oh I had a bath today and let my mind wander
down the coming year.
It looks warm and inviting.

7 Grattan Place 2010

A Child

It takes a thousand times
a thousand answers
to raise a child.

To hear and tend
the million questions
a small and growing mind can think off.

Not to mention
all the hints and shouts and sighs
and eyebrows raised
that form the guiding steps
to make a human being.

No no
don't do that.
Yes
Yes you can do that.

Good boy.
You are a really good girl.

A child is not a fawn
that follows feet and keeps in tow.
A wordless gangly calf
an egg left in a nest.

Sentience is hewn
tenderly and long
years upon year
smile by smile.

Frown by frown.
Word upon word
framed in the
intricate sentences of the face.

And hugs and kissy gestures
and warmly buttoned coats.

The gaze of a mother
on a child sucking
milk from deep and warm
within the blood.

A cradle rocked
to a lullaby.

A story every night before
falling soft asleep.

It takes a million answered questions
to raise a child.

A thousand times
a thousand answers.

All of them
        really   really
              important.

Grattan Place Freemans Bay 2009

Three Gifts

There can never be a lack of hope, ever.
Not because hope springs eternal
or that it is intrinsic to human nature.
It's simply that the human situation
always changes. It is never the same.
Even from minute to minute.
In this ever changing circumstance
there is always hope.

Charity can never be absent or lacking.
Even the poorest man can give you a smile.
And destitution need not be of the heart.
For charity is not merely giving.
Its gift lies in giving someone else
 the opportunity to give.

There can never be a lack of faith.
And this is not to say
that faith is perennial or ever present.
Just that the future is always upon us.
We can have absolute faith
that we have a future.

The decision as to the kind of future we will
have is ours and God's concern

As long as he has faith in us
We will have a future.

The return of Mars, non-criminals, unstolen goods and other portended undisasters.

By Wednesday
all the crisis's had passed away in time
and were no more.

The burglars never broke into the house
so there was not the need to scour West
Auckland flea markets for one's humble
chattels.

And Mars returned to earth
 without a word of where he had been
 or with who.

 and so

There was no need for a funeral
or to summon to mind
a vague memory of what he looked like.

As he was right there in purrson.
Dandering about in his usual haunts.

So all the worry,
all that worry.

Well that was the only thing real
about the crisis's.
The mountain of worry started to fade away.

Though still some worry persisted.

Being as how the original frenzied concern
over the impending disasters
that were never were to be
was so elevated and distraught
naturally the denouement
lingered in the mind for days.

All we can really do
I suppose
in the face of such conjured fear
and worried concern.
Is to praise the God of unexpected
consequences
for the peace and quiet he bestows
on those who wait
until disaster strikes
before
freaking out about it.

7 Grattan Place November 2009.

To be Irish - is to remember the famine

Deep in the marrow of the heart's soul
comes the visions
Wreathing out of the cold gray skies.
of long ago.

Starving children
stomachs distended
eyes , running with tears
 wailing   piercing   shrieking
along the roads of shame.

Their mothers praying for death
and the end of misery.
That their prayers might take them from hell
on earth
and raise them and all they loved to paradise.

Fathers, gaunt, death, a breath away
helpless to protect and feed
their own.

Two million innocent hearts.
Dying   in   agony.

To be Irish is to remember the Famine.
And ask God
to seek to so arrange the world
that it never happens
 to anyone   ever   again.

Southern River Perth WA February 2008

Running from Goma

She is running down the road
with a child under her arm.
Another child
holding her hand
is running along side,
screaming.

Back up there
her husband
is firing a machine gun
at people he hates.

They hate him back.
They are firing at him.
The town is in ruins.
Everything they own is destroyed,
in rubble, smelling of cordite
and hatred.

It's expensive
hatred.
Costs the earth

Love
love's for nothing.
And priceless
priceless
beyond measure.

Adelaide 2003

I feel death

I feel death's
deliberate fingers
reaching for me.

Not with the warm grip
of an old friend
with fond memories
to say hello
and shake my hand.

Nor with the fresh hand
of a new acquaintance
feeling out my sympathies
working round my sensitivities.

I feel death
taking a grip upon me.
The embrace will be
total final
and inevitable.

I had not thought
to feel the first tendrils
of his reaching arms
so soon.

At Glenn's Adelaide 2003

An Artist at work

The old man was an artist on the digger.
With one smooth fluid movement
he could swing that bucket
in under the power lines
down into the trench
over a bit of pipe and bring it down
with a resounding thump,
smack dab where it should be.

On a Traxie
he could scrape a batter
or curve a road
with the precision of a chef
sculpting icing on a cake.

He could reach in under the trees
and hoist them into the air
and with a rounding turn
drop them all in the 20 yard truck
as though they had never been.

He could get the five yard bucket
and smash every timber
in the side wall of a house
with one blow,
wrenching the joists apart
and loading the rubbished wall into a heap
as he waited for the truck to arrive.

The house gone in an hour.
Leaving bare scraped weedless ground
where once were paths and clothes lines
and rose bushes where children played.

He was an artist, with the power of his arms
and thighs multiplied a hundred thousand
times.

Doing what twenty men
might do in a day
in one hour.

The old man was an artist on the digger.

Demolition 8 Sandery Ave Seacombe Gdns 2003

Land Sea and Air

If I were the land
I would lie down
and let the tendrils of the ocean
teach me my edges.

I would fill the sea with lava
and push the waters hem
with sand and silt
out past the tide.

If I were the sea
I would rage
against the walls of the land
and wrench the soily flesh
into my wildest waves.

If I were the wind
I would blast the land
drench it with salt
and scour its skin
to gaping wounds.

yet

If I were the land
I would waft blossoms
down my rivers
as garlands to the sea.

Were I the sea
I would caress the shores with sweet wave
whispers in the night.

Were I the air
I would softly coat the grass
With the feathered lilt
of glistened rain.

Myself

I wish the peace of one
long Summers day.

At the side of the ocean.
At the edge of the ground.
At the winds beginnings.

At the Train Park Adelaide 2001

The Wave

When you died
on the sand
there was no sign
of where you had come from.
What your origins were.

Maybe from an iceberg
sliding into the freezing sea.

Perhaps a chance wind,
or a quirk of the current
deep in the southern ocean.

Taking your place in the procession
your white tops
scragged back in the screaming wind.
Were you a raging child
of the roaring forties?

At night
did you see the Southern Cross
glistening
in the dark cold sky?

When dawn broke and the sun
beamed from the east
was it warm on your thousand mile furl?

Gathering your strength
over the deep drenched blue
could you see the squid
and the tuna flashing
in the depths below you?

Did you know
the land was nearing?

That this immense Australia
barred your way?

I choose you specially.

I looked out for you
among the others.

Pushing my board into your shoulder
carving down your face
taking your speed and strength as mine.

When I mounted your back
for that last furled run to the sand.

Did you know your end was near.
Foaming
Splattering your way
to a death
in the sand,
in this place.

For Glenn Marion Adelaide 2001

82

For Oleg

A thousand years ago
we would have met on a hillside
in the quarter light of evening.

Sat in the growing winters dark.
Horses stamping in the cold
fire flickering through the birches.

Talked of life beyond the river
and compared places
we'd been drunk in.

Caravans with amber
from the forests end.
Met,
and made acquaintance
A thousand years ago.

A hundred years ago.
In a coffee house or quiet pub,
the lamplights gleam across a table.
The warm snug damp of day,
washed away in the froth of a pint.

A throng pressed up against the times
concerns.
Ships and trades
rolling round the room.
A hundred years ago.

I cannot ride a horse
across the sea
and see your eyes
or place your hand in mine
nor wander every town
 to seek you there
and hear your voice.

The rivers far away,
the ships
bear castled boxes,
out beyond the waves.

We met behind a screen,
words flung across the world and time
as careless as a straw
blown down a city street.

Our screens
glow separate and afar
but through the tangled web we came
past the obstacles of time and space.

and in that place

we may well count ourselves

well met.

Adelaide Feburary 1999

Icons

Give us your representations,
No anguish dear
just the pure abstraction

Give us your art, the text perhaps.
We can interpret it, deconstruct it
reconstruct it
without your appalling grammar
your smell.

Your food, send your food
just the ingredients dear
we'll rework them
preferable on porcelain.

No, not you
nor your snotty children.
Give us designs graphical interpretations
icons please, motifs if possible.

No not the dust, the grime
the misery.
We can't sell that
Send us reports on your agony.
We can represent you.
Get programs in place.

But no,
don't come to the office
or call by home.

Adelaide February 1998

Looking For God

I met a man the other day
who said
he was looking for God.

I said, "look mate
 Maybe
 if you hadn't lost him in the first place
 you wouldn't be chasing him now."

"Yes," he said
"maybe," he said
"but I need him now."

"He has to be somewhere",

"Well," I suggested
"maybe he's on Alpha Centauri
maybe its all happening there."

"Oh," he said, "but I need him here."

"Maybe,"I said, "maybe he's got Alzheimer's.
He is getting on you know
Or perhaps, he just forgot about you."

"Hmmn," he said. "Thats a point."

"More likely," I said,
"he's talking to Bob Dylan."

"You mean," he said,
"Bob Dylan talks to God."

"That's not what I said, In fact
its the other way round."

"Oh," he said, "Then I should find Bob Dylan."

"Well," I said, "That would be harder."

"Look," I said,
"wait a bit.
A good while
have patience
a lifetime perhaps
and
maybe
God will find you.

Adelaide 1998

Courage

She is bent over her stick
haunched into the wind
struggling up the road
to buy a few small things
in the shop.

One push
her purse
her life
gone.

Any dog can shake her
like a rag.

Why is it
the awards for courage
go to the fit
and not the frail.

She's brave.
Brave
beyond
imagining.

Adelaide January 1997

88

Donagh Cross

In the smoky corner of a cottage,
she's in a chair.
Braiding the tears of children
into a small crocheted hat.
Yellow whins - blue lake - green sward
Woven into a silver tweed.

Boys
laughing under a hedge.
Girls
flying down the road.
Tinkers arguing the price of horses
where long ago chieftains met.

O'Neills, Maguires, Armstrongs and Clarks.
all in their time
made lives in these small fields.
Stooked corn between the walls.

Pikes flailing, gunfire spitting
bombed bridges on the Finn.
Cara house in ruins.
hatred rattling every stone.

Christ, the Christ
of all the Christians
bring peace.

Adelaide 1997

89

Cara House Newtonbutler

Cara lies in ruins.
Shame guttering down the slates.
Below the house
the border runs along the road
hatred minding every hazelled mile.

The Finn glides to the Erne.
A fox sidles through the laurel.
The orchard is totally silent.
Cara's ruins wait for peace.

Across the world we call down difference
and set aside the future.
Take up new quarrels
to mine the emenity of days gone by.
Dig up the dead, fling the stone.
Bow the head to the ancestors.

Generations learn again
the grudges of the past.
once again, once again

This is our country,   We are one people
  I am not like you   You are not indigenous
          We are different religions
            You do not belong here
We are different   I am different
You are different   They are different

Your forefathers murdered mine
Mine murdered yours
This is our land   This is our land
For your dead fathers deeds kneel in shame
We have nothing in common

Love your enemies
forgive the dead
Honour them
bury them.

I was born here.
So was I.
I belong here
so do I

In my minds eye I see
the hare rise from the rushes
a greyhound lope
across the windy fields.

Below the elms
snowdrops nod
green
and triumphant.

And soft beneath the snow
the shamrock waits
for Patrick's day.

Adelaide 1997

What an odd quad

The other day behind my screen

I met a man I've never seen.

He might drop in again today.

I wonder what he'll have to say.

Adelaide February 1997

Without you

If we didn't have you
the house would be so tidy.

All the floors would gleam.
There'd be no books
scattered everywhere.
If you weren't about
it would be so quiet
and peaceful and so, so calm.

If we didn't have you
we could go out more.
We'd have times to ourselves.
There's so many things we could do.

But if we didn't have you
we'd miss all your joy
your happy sparkling eyes
your laughing in the hall.

If we didn't have you
we'd miss every little flower that you admire
all the words you found
all the questions
all the happiness you bring.

If you weren't here we would miss so much.

every little grubby mark
and every scattered sock
is a blessing.

Oh a world without you
would be joyless
and sterile and clean indeed.

Adelaide 1997

Nua.ie

It was swift fingers lifted us from the bog.
Deft, vellum smoothed, fingers
the oily dyes foundered into them.
Gnarled fingers of the hands of saints.

It was keen eyes, squinting over the letters
pondering meaning,
the minds wandering
penned words slowly ensnared into scrolls.
Weaving across the brightling page
the very words of God.

It was clever tongues
that rolled the dreams of Gaels
through the language of the strangers.
Shone Eirean's light
through cruel days
cloud shadows on the fields.

Till now
in these glow of screens,
trolling the webs of imagination.
we hold hands across the world.

Wefting a future
for the children of Eire,
scattered no more.

Adelaide 1996

Belair

At breaking day
before
the sun's bright gold
was flung
among the bird shrilled gums.

I saw a kangaroo
bronze red
against the green
dewed turf.

We met

as friends of old.

He stood

belonging

perfectly.

Belair Golf Course Adelaide 1996

Adelaide – The Birds of Morning

Sun up.
The singing armies of the morning
mobilise noisly across the dry burnt fields.

Cape pigeons strut on parade.
Prussian spiked heads bobbing
among the grass heads.

Major Mitchells red waisted colonel blimps
with white cockades heads throdding
hold manoeuvres in the flowers.

Blackbirds scouting
three steps - stop - listen - three steps again.

Quail riders of dispatch hurry
purpose plain.
Swallows aerial spies
wheel swift round the fields rim.

Doves coo retreat
preachy parrots screech reproach
and threaten fisticuffs.

I am conductor
of the of the feathered force.
My movements change the trill.
My strides crescendos silence.
I am commander of the song.

Adelaide 1998

Adelaide - Summer Morning

The sun
slants out across Murray plains.
and angles up behind the eastern hills
teasing out the mists among the trees
and spreads a golden syrup
down each bird fledged valley.

Sand stones
glow bronzed in shale
until the light shafts crown the gum lined sky.

Steeples kiss the breathless air.
The gardens gown the streets.
Park - flower – hedge
rustle to the fingered brightness.

The beaches yellow taunt the oceans edge.
Adelaide rises
pleasant, cultured content.

The sun
framed for evening now
glances fire.
across the water
to the hushing shore.

Adelaide 1996

Adelaide – Autumn's Leaves

The nights breeze made such a party.
Crowdy bands of dancers
mad for one last heedless fling.

A bustling wind drove swirling throngs
throstling, swishing,
rasping, flittering
mad merry helpless in the air.

By late afternoon
tired ragged windgone little crowds
weary heaps of bronzy yellow rouge
gatherings in corners
shouldered up against the grassy verge
piled sleepy bands of crispy peace.
tired of dancing.

The low skies sun
casts long shadows on the eucalyptus
swaggering glossy grey green sheened leaves
not for us they say, oh not for us.

And from the cherry ash
the leaves have gone

Embarrassed in the branches
bare fingered now against the blue
revealed the dove's last summers nest
the tiny brood
reared and gone.

Adelaide 1996

For Rory   (and the Ants)

Sometimes
when you're eating dinner
the ants are looking in,
to see what's going in the bin.

Oh what a feast
we'll have tonight
they say.

Look
Rory hasn't eat his greens.
Danny hasn't eat his beans
and Keifer's left his meat.

So
lets keep the ants
healthy and thin.

And make ourselves wealthy,
make ourselves winners,
by eating
all our dinners.

For it's no matter the weather,
the ants get together,
get into a bunch ,
and go out to lunch
to dine in the big green bin.

Listen,
listen, hard
and you'll hear
Ant mothers say.

"Don't never,
not ever
eat out on a Thursday night"

"It was one Thursday back
that your uncle Jack
went out for a snack
and never came back
Alas and alack!!

The bin was took out
he was shook out the spout
and went away with the muck
in a big rubbish truck
and was never
ever
seen again.
Ever.

Daddy 1996

Details

The sign said they were mobile "detailers".
I thought this is wonderful.
I've been after a detailer for some time.
I rang them up

I said look.
I have heaps of details that need looking after.
The house is full of them.
Nagging details, important details.
Could you come round and fix them up.
Attend to them?

He said "no they only detailed cars."
I said "look if I had a car I could detail it
myself"
Its the important details that need a detailer

You would wonder wouldn't you.
Imagine a van
to rush around attending to the details of cars
What fecking details do cars have anyway.

While the really important ones.
The details that matter
have no one, no one,
to attend them at all.

Celtic Avenue Clovelly Park 1996

In the English Channel

I am coming home tonight
across a dark and drowsy sea
to your warm arms
beyond the edges of the waves.

I send my love
myself soon follows.

Along the starboard side
gleaming yellow buildings
Ostend Calais Dunkerque.

Their golden lights become
nothing
darkness.

Then
glittered on the port
Deal Sandwich and Dover.

Over the heights
and red lit towers
are you and Danny.

For Jill. 29 June 1989.

For Squiggles

You know squiggles
When I go up the road
and disappear beyond the furthest lamp post
that you can see.

I go to a world
of phones and confusion
that you can have no part of.

And in that world Squiggs
they are amassing hate
at such a pace
that one day Squiggs
in a flash of malice.

They'll destroy
all the butterflies
that you have chased
and all the friends
that you have made
and all the garden smells
that you've explored.

So   ...   If you hear that rumble Squiggs
and if the ground shakes Squiggs
and if your eyes catch fire Squiggs.

Don't forgive them Squiggles
Don't   forgive them
ever.

Franklin Rd Ponsonby 1982

Coming to the PSA Advisory Council

Coming down here
on the plane
the white quilts of fog
were clothing the west of Taranaki.

In Taumaranui,
the trees stretched their arms
to the waiting mist
still gathering up his cloaks
and dancing away from the
still blinking sun.

Wellington is dark under cloud.
But the shining fire will come down the Hutt
and
break the clouds soon.

July 4th 1982

Franklin Road

The old man marches his dreams
past the Ponsonby bus stop
up, and down.
He's as mad as a rabbit
and every one knows it
but him.

The bus takes us down Franklin Rd.
A van takes him to Carrington.
Not many years ago
he was much like the rest of us
till the niceness arrived.

The 7 o clock bus carts off the workers
All brown and bedraggled off to the factories
to make the goodies they cannot afford.

The King Cobras are angry and sullen and
grievanced.
They weren't on the bus.
They'll make do for the rest of the day
welcome at Andy's and no other place.

Later this morning
when we have all gone.
Our new masters and mistresses
will take to the streets.
to drink lattes.

They wont miss us a bit.
They won't even know we have left.

23 Franklin Road Ponsonby 1981

Adam's Cats

You would think,
sometimes,
that
all over the world.

There's a conspiracy of Cats.
Sitting at front gates.
Passing news of some war
or other human affair
or a new set of kittens
Up
and
down
the street.

1981 In the Falklands War

Spring 1984

It's so slow.

A flower here

a chase of sparrows there

a warming day

and now returning

the boastful sun.

At the Department of Statistics 1979

Adam's Kittens

Well
Kittens
You arrived suddenly.
Blinking eyes of amazement.

Last time I was here you were not.

Now,
you are furry little raiders
pouncing ambushes beside my face.
Tumbling down
the sleeping bag
through all the clutter.

You're the delight
Of a windy morning.
A magic
of the world's real charm.

At Adam Gifford's house Haitaitai Wellington 1981

Muldoon

These islands at the end of the earth
Live in a dreary fascination with the past.

Terrified of a world pushed on them
from above the equator.
Afraid of a world they feel helpless to change.

The short sighted fat dwarf
towers over the landscapes of our horizons
battering us to a sullen
myopic vision of towers
and steel and chemical plants.

We are poor among plenty.

Yet the land is rich.
The soil as productive as ever.
The sun shines as often.
The people are as clever as before.

Its the social soil that has for the moment
turned sour and barren.
We bow to the dwarf and his minions.

If the last war comes
these islands
will be the last place on earth.

It could be better than this.

Hopetoun Street Ponsonby 1978

For Donal

I'd like to make me a person I could like
and live with all my life.
A person of my construction whom I could
in my own sense
be proud of.

I'd like my creation to be me.

Not my only achievement but at least
one of my principle constructions.

I shouldn't like there to be two mes.
One the shop store window front.
The other,
 the private apartment of my faith.

I would prefer
there was one
I.

Ministry of Works Friday 26 July 1974

At 97

I speak to you
from a generation that is dead.

As one
who made the world
when you were young.

I made the world
from the dreams
of my youth.

Be very
very
careful
when you dream.

For the world of today
is but the dreams of our youth
made into reality.

Bledisloe Building Auckland 1974

On the Train To Oxford

Nothing saddens me more
than marching soldiers
or marble memorials
to the dust of worms
to the honour of God.

How brave to die
so stupidly.

To be remembered by stark lies
in bronze writing.

"Greater love no man hath"

"Dulce et decorum est pro patria mori."

Whit Weekend 1968

Harry and Cecilia

Tea with Charlie Chequers
dinner with the Ponds.
Up to the Randolph
Down to Carfax.

Cecilia Harry
Harry Cecilia.

All the people you have talked to
all the faces brushed upon
will soon be memories.

Yet years from now
the children of your children's children
will flash your eyes.

and

someone, somehow
will catch a glint
of some remembered touch
Or glance or whisper.

Feel a tender
Feeling.

And wonder.

Oxford 1968

The Stranger

He became informed
for himself only.
Oh for mankind also
but only to himself spoke it.

He was tortured
breathing syllables
unheard in the normal air.

The eyes beaming out
without reflection
on themselves glared
in the end.

He knew himself
as a universe
untrampled.

And in the other world
he kneeled in affliction.

In the end
his soul seeped out
and was lost
in the wash of humanity.

For Kem Cason
On the Cap Finnesterre 1967

Graffiti

God loved graffiti.
He wrote it
on walls in the world.
Pasted up pictures
on the leaves of hushed morning.

Wrote love
on crisp white sand
among reeds.

So

cover this wall with beads of enchantment.
A personal embroidery
of the souls lost streams.

Slivers of time,
lost gone
on the mills of our hurry.
Leave here
loves tribute
to the hearts
true
friends.

For the Karapiets San Francisco 1967

Big Sur

The waves here
rage careless on the shore.
In abrasive consternation
on these rough uncaring bays.

Rage on Sea.
You will not prevail against this hinterland.
Sea, you are relegated to an economic asset.
All around rests the land
capriciously, organised into insensitivity.

Private property.
No Trespassing.
A dollar toll to use this road.

How can they buy the sea and sky?

They would vend the sun if
they could can the light.

Big Sur July 7 1967
For Country Joe and the Fish.

Sea Island

I should like to live by an airport
and watch the big jets
glide gracefully along the runways of the sky.

I would feel near to the Indies.
There
in the outflung suburbs.

Right next to Delhi and Shannon.
Watching these giant things

come
    down
        down
           thump
              thump
                bump

                        On the ground.

I would like to live by the sea.
The long night slumbering sea.
That lisps its way in the dark
to the hushing shores.

And dream, that out there,
beyond the furthest cloud,
lay the sea of Japan.

September 15 1967   Sea Island Vancouver

The Old Men

The old men
are dragging the world to destruction.
And the old women are cheering them on

They are asking us
to march behind them
to oblivion.

They are defending
the relics of their anger and stupidity.
They are insane.

They have poisoned us
with their malevolence.

They want us to hold the weapons.
To feel them
and know their power.

They want us
children
to share their shame.

March 1966
At the Golden Cross
Waitekauri
Waihi.

Wet Steers

God, who sent this day?
The winds cracking like a whip round the ridge.
The rain's set in for days.
Its wet and cold.
The sheep have draped themselves
at the trees edge.
You weren't fast of the chain
this morning, were you dog?

You're saying "it is all my fault", dog.
Well the trucks due at four mate.
There is nothing else for it.

Come on Tui, Queen.
We've ten steers to get from that wet green
dripping bush at the top of the gully.

Its rain like this would drives a man
to an office desk.

The hell it would.
Shake yourself dogs.
Come on horse.
get your head into the wind.
We're at it.

Waitekauri
Waihi 1966

On Lines of Faulkner.   Sanctuary

As falcons make love in falling space,
In falling rhyme to break and wheel away in
separate dawn.

They splice their wonder
in the fleeting wings
and then make love
in falling space.

All love
this windy nest
on craggy sky.

A fruitfulness of instincts love.
Ordained in symphony.

Derelicts on charted shores.

"and all a man can do is take his hat and coat
and walk away."

For Richard Townsend
1965 Mt Roskill .

Notes on Poems

For times to come
What if you have a really dangerous idea, What do you do?

The Alone crowd
Written a few yearsd ago but niow the idea is well explained in the Book "Party of One - The loners' Manifesto". I like being alone.

The Policy
The elitist makers of the plans and those they plan for. planned for increases year by year.

Riches in a book
Surfing the internet one wet sunday I saw a book, "Before you go" by the Dublin City Corpfor a Dublin street guide for tourists. The book described the poets, singer, writers and songwriters who had graced the city. I sent them this poem which they put on their web site.

Walking
I was walking down Swanson Road towards Henderson and all of a sudden it occurred to me how many associations I had with the place where my feet stood.

A blessed Land
It is a fine view from Slievenamon. The mountain of women. "Where nature has lavished her bounty." as the song goes.

The Recipe
My mother had a recipe for wheaten bread. it's in the poem. But the recipe is not the making of it. And that was something that only my mother could do well. Fried in butter and bacon grease with an Ulster Fry it was the food of paradise.

What is
Half the woprld seems confused about the reality it lives in. What is about them. despite what you hear from the postmodernists What is actually is.

Notes on Poems

Wellington

I like Wellington. The drama isn't only in the weather. It is full of vibrant people and valleys hidden with tenaciousness and verve.

The Music

I learnt Irish dancing from Alice Whitty in Turakina Street in Auckland in the 50's. A dancer has a different relationship to music formed in the body. I have been fortunate to travel in music from the prairies of Neil Young to the waltzs of Galicia. From the dry Cardrona to Derry.
All songs are poems given atmospheres of sound that bathe us in every emotion from pathos to love, delight and longing.

The Wren

There is a brave adventurousness among so many of the birds of the hedge and woods. The Willy Wagtail, the Thrush, Blackbird, Robin Red Breast and the bands of finches that traipse through the grass and meadows. The wren is the King of the birds, the small emperor of cheerfulness and hope.

The Hedge at Clonmel

I spent my young years peering in and about the hedges of the townlands of Cara, Clontiveret and Essnadarragh. It was a wonderland of hazels rods damson plums, The sedges and streams and above all the birds were entrancing. I fell in love with the Irish countryside then and so again these many years later.

The Founder of the State.

Ships founder and so do states. The foundation of the Republic of Ireland was a remarkable and heroic achievement. It has so much potential. The hatreds are hopefully passing away into memory.

Melike the cat.

Melike is Jose's cat in the beautiful city of Salamanca. He was a nice cat but pined when Jose left the flat. He had a great wish to see the world outside and lived a cloistered life much like the humans do these days. They have their screens and cats their toys.

Over there

I was reading Seamus Heaney's remarks in "Participations" borrowed on Danny 'O' Donnell's library card from the Clonmel library and read a piece on a sense of place.

A sense of place is different for everyone but peculiarly so for people from Northern Ireland. I remembered my experiences as a boy being taken across the frontier to a country not yet 50 years of age from a province barely a year older. It was to experience strangeness among a people so recently divided.

Adam

Was a fine young Englishman I met in Jose's in Salamanca. He had an idea he would like to become a spy. He was returning to complete a degree in African Studies and he seemed to have the wit and determination to make a good Intelligence officer.

Mare Nostrum

I had read a lot of history about the place I was now in. And it struck me how knitted together this world was by the Mediterranean. To the Romans it was simply Our Sea.

Le Fly

One fine day in the Cannes apartment this small fly started doing aerobatics. He was tireless. I was so aware of his location, in France and that I was a foreigner and he was not.

Le Fly II - The roomy

The fly was still about a day later. Getting comfortable, making himself at home.

Le Fly III - Trouble

It was all getting out of hand.

The Coast road

I was sitting in Caannes thinking about my journey back to New Zeland when it occurred to me how nice it would be to go up that coast again. Funds would not allow it but it's on the bucket list.

Cote de Azur

There were these two doves used to come into the apartment and clean up the crumbs. Demure and dainty and head nodding businesslike about their task Cannes is Nice and Nice is nicer.

In Cannes

I lived for a short time on the Boulevard Alexander III in the Californie district of Cannes. It was quite magical.
The land behind Cannes on up to Grass was beautiful.

Air New Zealand Flight 035

From Hong Kong to London. It is an astonishing flight. I loved every minute of it.

A Day came

I was staying in Surrey with Thomas Forde, a man from Mayo lately of Thomas Fordes Bar and Political museum in Anzac St Auckland.
It struck me how rare a day is with out plans for it. .

Flutterby Butterfly

I was walking across from the Embassy theatre at the end of Courtney Place Wellington, in early February.

The sun was out and past my shoulder flew this butterfly wafting in and out of the shops, under the trees around the bus stops and the toilets without a care in the world.

They love you Still

I was in Dunedin recently. A fine and friendly town. I sat in the Church of John Knox and wondered at the virtue and decency of the settlers who came so far to make a town and province. And yet these good Presbyterians put a poet in the centre of the town. A man who drank and loved women.

I am fond of Burns poetry especially the songs and the magic airs used to frame the poesy in music. The strains of Annie Laurie sung by the Corries is one of my very favourite tunes.

A Prayer for Caroline

Caroline is entranced with words. And is a devotee of the 26 letters of the alphabet and how they form into words and meanings and the meanings held in between the words.

And loves the 24 hours of the day into which words and we must fit.

God and the Ants

I was walking across the parkland on the south side of the centre of Adelaide.

I had for a number of years wondered why there were so many sorts of Ants. I put it down to God having too much time on his hands.

The small dinosaurs

I have come to love sparrows.

They so bravely rise in the morning with neither house or income.
In the summer they have a tribe of constantly pleading offspring to feed. Yet they tackle the task of existing in our complicated cities with bravado and chutzpah.

The dinosaurs live on now as birds of the air. If you look at the sparrows and imagine them with scales they are indeed small dinosaurs. And they have learnt to sing.

The Tide turns.

I suppose there are elements of the "tipping point" here.
I worked hard for a number of years on political ideas.

Nuclear free New Zealand was one. All is against you until one day the tide turns. It seems that the world comes to pass in rhythms and surges."

The Dark awaits

Just came into my head on a flight across the Tasman.
No particular reason and no explanation. I wrote it out on a Lan Chile napkin.
It was a good flight and the staff on the plane were nice.

I had a bath today.

I was staying with my good friend, John Langdon (RIP), in Freemans bay and the plastic bath was broken by some heavyweight acquaintance of John's.

A Child

Rearing, raising children involves a lot of questions and in times past children had attentive ears to answer those questions.

The wisdom of ancestors is passed down the generations in this simple fashion.

Three Gifts

I do believe that good does prevail. It is still here. It has never really been defeated. We know so little about the workings of the world and the cosmos.

But I do have faith that our children and their children on to forever will slowly make the world a better place.

Mars the Cat.

A relative of a friend went overseas and left my friend with the duty of minding the cat and seeing the house was not pillaged.

The cat, Mars, vanished and the hysteria about what could have happened to him was monumental.

The alarm was that he and all the goods in the house could have been stolen. Why the burglars would take a stroppy cat was a strange notion.

As it happened the thieves must have had better houses to burgle and the cat, well Mars decided that if the "owners" were going to bugger off he too might as well take a holiday and he wandered off for a foray into the wilds of Freemans Bay.

In all good time Mars sauntered back. There was no burglary. I was thinking that the world is full of hysteria about things that never happened, were never likely to happen and events we cannotimagine that will happen.

To be Irish

The famine in one way or other has seared all Irish minds.

Along with the joys of our songs and gaiety is the 700 years of the sorrows.

No calamity of the many in Irish History is more stark and devastating than the famine.

Running From Goma

I took this from a picture in the paper of a woman in terror running from the burning town of Goma in the Congo.
Some band of brigands were fighting a dictatorship funded and fuelled by overseas aid. Why we pay the hard earned earnings of hard working citizens to help African dictators to treat their citizens with utter contempt is a mystery.

I feel Death

Written in Glenn Norman's pottery in Adelaide.

We were talking and I felt a distinct touch of mortality.
A strange and chastening feeling.

An artist at work

I have in my many occupations had the opportunity to see machine operators at work. I drove a traxcavator in England and was a dab hand at loading trucks.

Even as you know the physics behind hydraulics there is a magic and a mystery why the flick of a wrist can send five yards of bucket high over the side of a truck.

I was watching an old man on a five yard digger smash a wooden house to shreds in half an hour and clean the entire lot up trees, garden and all into a heap.

The old codger was so skilled and fluidic in the way he handled that large machine that it was true artistry in all its aspects.

Land Sea and Air

I wrote this in a small park in Melrose Park in South Adelaide in one sitting while my children played on the train playground.

The first part of the poem tries to see the interfaces between the land sea and air from a "fierce" point of view as such interactions often are.

The second part looks at the soft relationships the wind sea and air do also have.

I was remembering my favourite place and magic days along the coast between Kari Kari and the Pararaha valley on Auckland's west coast.

The Wave

I made only one friend in my years in Adelaide. Adelaidians are standoffish people.
Glenn Norman was a potter and a surfer and from New South Wales.
I listened as he tried to give me the feeling it is to mount a wave and ride it to the shore.

I am trying to see the wave as it comes to Glenn. Alas Glenn died at the age of 48. He's catching all the perfect waves up there I am sure.

For Oleg

I made friends with a chap Oleg in Russia on the Internet. We exchanged views and notions on all sorts of things.

We live in a cyber world where people gain their idea of reality from television and the Internet.

I think the reality of their neighbourhoods and all about them eludes them.

I wondered how this different kind of friendship would compare to how people met and made friends in times past.

Icons

The billions of dollars spent annually by Australians taxpayers at the behest of "caring" lefties is destroying with welfare a people who survived with dignity for 40,000 years in one of the world's harshest environments.

These latté socialists with their aboriginal paintings on the wall would treat with disgust the victims of their state charity were they to call at their doors.

Looking for God

I did meet a chap once who asked me where to find God.
It seemed a strange question in Adelaide, the city of churches.

Stranger to me when it seemed that the maker of the cosmos could be anywhere and everywhere.

Don't they teach catechism any more? Where is God. God is everywhere.

That said I wonder if there are places even the most high God would rather not be?

Courage

Just a passing thought that a lot of honours for courage go to fit young men in their prime while an old woman in any part of the world can take her life in her hands on a walk to the shops with frail limbs and aching joints.

I think that's courage.

Donagh Cross.

Donagh is a small village near the Lisnaskea to Clones Road in Co Fermanagh. When we came to the crossroads at Donagh we knew we were on our way to see my mother's people up in the "mountains" at Essnadarra near Roslea.

My mother and five of us children left Cara House near Newtonbutler in March 1956 to join my father in New Zealand.

Cara House

We lived in Cara house before we came to New Zealand. It had its own woods, orchard, rookery, acres of green Irish land, a laurel grove and 10 or 20 rooms including a ball room. It was a mansion of the old ascendency.

It has struck over the years since the reconstruction of history began in the 1970's that New Zealand is hell bent on righting the "wrongs" of the 1800's.

I am gladdened for Northern Ireland by the remarks of the Grandmaster of the Orange Lodge a few years ago.

"We must forget the past wrongs on all sides. Let bygones be bygones." There is no future in the past.

An odd Quad

A rather childish reference to the Cambridge exchange between idealistic and empirical philosophers.
Has the Internet changed it?

Without You

My daughter Tracie who seemed to leave the house bestrewn with socks prompted me to consider what was the real problem.

An untidy house was a very small sacrifice for have such a charmingly beautiful child bring us so much joy.

Nua.ie

www.nua.ie was an internet site in Ireland. I had become enchanted with the Internet in 1994 while I worked as the Retail Manager at Auckland International Airport.

McGovern was one of the early pioneers of the Internet in Ireland and set up the web site Nua and was a mentor to many.

It occurred to me that the long 2,500 year heritage of the Celtic Irish would thrive on the Internet and provide them with the means of connecting across the world.

Belair

When my wife Jill and our four children arrived in Adelaide in 1996 we stayed at a camping ground in the Belair National Park. A wondrous place.

I had been led to settle in Adelaide by the promise by the State Government that Adelaide was to be the wired city of the southern hemisphere, the Athens of the south.

Like all expensive government visions of the future it turned out to be a myth.

I was walking early in the morning at the top end of the Belair Golf course and there standing on the green was a giant red Kangaroo.

He looked at me with that languid look that Kangaroos give intruders in their terrain.

Framed red against the rising sun on the green green sward of the golf course he so belonged.

Adelaide - Autumn leaves.

Adelaide is a beautiful city. Trees include cherry ashes and a lot of European deciduous trees and the leaves in autumn cascade across the streets and parks.

The swirling of the leaves and their drifting heaps beside the green grass edges fascinated me.

Adelaide – Summer morning

The Adelaide hills are surely the prettiest back drop to any city anywhere. The light is sharp and crisp since humidity is often in the 20's.

Seeing the gardens and the trees of the hundreds of parks and tree lined streets in the still warm air before a coming hot day is magic.

Adelaide – The birds of morning.

I used to walk in the early morning around Marion and Seacombe Gardens. Australia is full of many many kinds of birds. Like all good Australians they are proud of themselves and their songs.

As I was walking they would move or hush and I would change the songs and the behaviours of the birds.

Rory and the Ants.

When we first came to Australia the ants were a source of constant wonder. There were countless varieties of these energetic little scavengers treating our rubbish as a smorgasbord

We seemed to throw a lot of food out and I tried to convince all and sundry that feeding these moochers was not to be encouraged.

There seemed a bit of justice however when the bins went to the city dump and these fellows left the property rather rapidly as the morning the rubbish truck went down the street.

Detailers

There were in Adelaide vans who would come and groom your car. Looking after the details of a car seemed less valuable than all the other details about the place.

We have of course an endless bunch of social engineers making us sort our rubbish and install the "proper" light bulbs but the really important matters have no payable people to solve them.

In the English Channel

I was travelling in England with my wife Jill and our eldest son Danny. I took a notion to travel on my own to Brussels for a day trip to wander around the Headquarters of the European Union. I wanted to see if it was the giant bureaucratic waste of time it threatened to be.

Going home to Whitfield near Dover the light fell away from the houses on the continental shore and as we approached England the small towns on the shore had their lights on.

Squiggles

In the early eighties I inherited the tenancy of 23 Franklin Road from Adam Gifford, complete with a punk rock band the "Androids", half of Ponsonby and my cat Squiggles.

Actually "my" cat is not the way it was, I was "Squiggles" human. Squiggles mother was Julie Andrews who belonged to Mark, Tall Tony's boyfriend.

The cold war was in full swing, Muldoon was Prime Minister and it looked as though New Zealand would never be
Nuclear weapon free. In the event of a thermonuclear war New Zealand would be one of the last outposts of civilisation. In a nuclear holocaust all the animals in the world would disappear and I wondered if they would ever forgive us.

The house had a wonderful garden lovingly built by Jan Newton. "Squiggs" loved basking in and wandering about it.
It seemed so wrong that her world should be destroyed with ours as hatred dragged the world to possible destruction

Coming Down to the PSA Advisory Council

I was at one time (1981) Chairman of the Public Service Association in Auckland and each month flew down to a national meeting of the Advisory Council of the PSA.

I have driven all over the central North Island on many many occasions. To see from the air the mists drifting across the valleys and the glimmers of the morning sun striking the bush clad hills and green hills of the farms is fascinating.

Franklin Road

I lived in Ponsonby an inner Auckland suburb (1978 to 1986) when it was a friendly knockabout slum with halfway houses hippies, punk rockers, Islanders, Maoris and poor decent Pakeha New Zealanders.

It became gentrified about the early eighties and filled with the snobs and crass materialists it houses today.

Martha's house was bought for $28,000 in 1981. Today it's for sale at well over 1.5 million.

Yea verily the madness of sinking the wealth of a country into wooden houses.

Adam's Cats

I stayed a few days at Adam Gifford's flat in Haitaitai in Wellington and was bemused by the habits of the cats in the district.

In the early morning as in St Stephens avenue in Parnell the Cats sat outside the gates of the houses watching up and down the road.

I used to take a walk with my cat Fred, up St Stephens Avenue and see him take the courage to litigate a few of his feuds with the neighbouring tomcats in the rich houses. Right little revolutionary was Fred.

Adam's Kittens

On another visit to Adam's in Wellington I woke up early one morning to find my self on the floor surrounded by a posse of playful kittens.

A few played "King of the Castle" while the rest staged assaults of low cunning and fake ferocity to gain the high ground near my shoulder.

It seemed to last for hours with unbounded energy.

My hair became a haystack they thought they could unravel and my toes a wiggling challenge worthy of little toothy fierceness.

Spring 1984

This was part of a number of poems I scribbled at my desk
when working at the Department of Statistics from 1978 to 1986.

I like sparrows. To me spring arrives on the day the cheeky feathered lot start
their mating chirrups and chases around the neighbourhood.

Muldoon

Prime Minister of New Zealand 1975 to 1984. he wrecked the New Zealand
economy, destroying the hope of generations.

Cancelled the Auckland underground "Robbie's Rapid Rail".
wiped out eight billion dollars in his "think big" projects and bullied the
population into a sullen silence.

With the usual injustice of politics Muldoon escapes the blame and it is firmly
affixed to those who repaired the damage. Oh and he subsidised the sheep flock
to 71,585,356 million sheep. Its about 35 million today.

I know.
I worked in the Department of Statistics at the time and was responsible for
counting them.

For Donal

I worked as a Legal clerk at the Ministry of Work in the Bledisloe Building in
downtown Auckland for a few years in the early seventies.

I resolved that I would always try and act the same no matter where I was and
no matter who I was talking to. Its not always socially wise

At 97

If I should I be so lucky to live that long. The ideals we form when we are
young can be a beacon of certainty in a chaotic world.

It took me years to understand that the world changes and while it is sensible
to set aside the misinformation in your view of the world and realign and
reinterpret the reality of now along side the principles you always hold.

Like any old curmudgeon I guess I am saying, think long and hard and dream
the best you can when you are young but as time goes by be prepared to change
your opinions but not your principles.
Have a dream but proceed from reality as my hero Deng Xiaoping was wont to
say.

On the train to Oxford

In 1968 I was in London. Occasionally I'd take the train to Oxford to see my cousin Sean Mulholland who was at Pembroke College. The train kept passing through small towns with their war memorials.

I was reminded of one of my favourite poems, Wilfred Owens's, Dulcie et Decorum est pro patria Mori" - How sweet and fitting it is to die for the fatherland.

I wished we had a world where no one died for any fatherland.

Harry and Cecilia

I lived in Oxford for a while, driving a taxi. I loved the town, the debates and talks with students. Harry had been a barber there in the 50's and made some dear friends, The Ponds and an artist called Charlie Chequers.

I came to understand abstraction and abstract art from Charlie explaining how his paintings of cups melting into a table were not representations but abstracts extracted from the "idea" of tables and cups.

I thought how many people Harry and Celia had touched and how their descendants would touch more.

The Stranger

Comes from conversations with a charming American, Kem Cason who hailed from Palatka Florida.

Kem, myself, my good friend Gary Fletcher and two Canadians from Saskatchewan worked our passage on the Columbus line ship "Cap Finisterre". We sailed from Sydney Australia around New Zealand calling at Hawaii and landing in Los Angeles on July 4th 1967.

Graffiti

Gary Fletcher and I landed in Los Angeles after our long voyage on the Cap Finnisterre.

We bought a small Pontiac in Los Angeles and drove up Highway 1 camping at Big Sur and Carmel.

We arrived in San Francisco just in time to greet the "Summer of Love". We stayed with Cecilia and Harry Karapiet, Gary's Aunt and Uncle in law in Daly City. Harry has had a major influence on my life.

I still have the copy of "A little Treasury of Modern Verse" edited by Oscar Williams, a gift from Harry.

He introduced me to classical music, Armenian culture and over many long discussions I came to understand his deep spirituality and his playful sentimentality.

He had a wall on which family mementoes, strange things that interested Harry and all sorts of intriguing items were placed.
I always try to have a "Harry's" wall wherever I live.

Big Sur

Gary Fletcher and I drove up Highway 1 from Los Angeles in July 1967 in a small Pontiac. We camped out for a few days at Big Sur above the small beach.

On the road as we drove down to the beach there was a sign saying there was a dollar toll to use the beach. This to our way of thinking was outrageous. The concept of owning a beach was beyond us.

There were about four types of climate as you climbed up the three mile long slopes from the beach up 1500 meters to the high alpine meadows. We lived with humming birds and a lot of wildlife we had never seen before.

The coast was enchanting with the waves flung against the soaring headlands and the mists of the morning weaving between the coast and pine lined sky

Sea Island Vancouver

After staying with the Karapiets in San Francisco we drove up to Vancouver and lived variously at Spanish Banks beach, sitting at the edge of a public beach much like Mission Bay in Auckland cooking over our primus.
We moved to Howe Sound and lived for a while in an idyllic paradise among chipmunks, squirrels and all sorts of astounding wildlife.
We swam in the sea until we found that the little strippey sea snakes were poisonous but carried on walking on water, a big log submerged beneath our feet anyway.

We were very poor. We picked blueberries on Sea Island near the Airport.

We made five dollars a day and spent it on bread and milk which was our sole diet, well, except that is for far too many blueberries. I loved seeing the jets come and go. I still love aircraft and flying.

The Old Men

I wrote this in 1966 at Waitekauri near Waihi. I owned a farm there in partnership with my brother Pat. Pat died of cancer in 1981. He is always missed.

I had read about the Aldermaston marches of the Campaign for Nuclear Disarmament (CND) in mid 1950s in the Daily Mirror, an English paper I read at the home of family friends Mickey and Cissie Wade at Paparata. (They made he "peace" symbol is that of the CND.)

I felt that the generation that had placed the world on 15 minute alert for the end of the world were dragging my generation into a maelstrom of hatred and insanity.

The end of the cold war has changed my thinking a little but it was a real feeling in those times.

Wet Steers

I owned a farm with my brother Pat at the Golden Cross Waitekauri, Waikino, Waihi.

I spent nearly all my time my bulldozer, (an International BTD6), but also managed with Pat 1200 sheep, 80 dry cattle and 60 milking cows not to mention pigs and far too many possums. I helped with the mustering.

We had a good young mare and great dogs, Queeny, Tui, an eye dog and one of the worlds finest cattle dogs, a Queensland Blue Heeler.
I was never as good as Pat with the stock whip but I could manage a horse with a stockman's saddle.

I wrote this after a day on my own, mustering cattle in the rain, The cattle had been in the bush a while and were as 'toey' and bloody uncontrollable.

The wet windy day left the dogs and horse with no enthusiasm for the job at all. But the truck was coming at four to take the cattle to the works so it had to be done.

On lines of Faulkner

I started writing poems about 1961. My first was about Sharpeville and the injustice of Mandela's jail

I have on various occasions lost nearly all my manuscripts, once in 1978 in San Francisco and again in the late 80's in Auckland.

This one survived from when I lived at 15 Subritzky Ave Mt Roskill. in Auckland and my good friend Richard Townsend was as I vaguely recall waxing rhapsodic on William Faulkner's book "Sanctuary."

The Author.

I was born in 1947 in County Fermanagh, Northern Ireland, and emigrated to New Zealand in 1956, aged 9.

I am a Citizen of Ireland, Australia, New Zealand and the United Kingdom.

I was educated at Moughly School, Clonmaulin School, St Josephs Convent, Grey Lynn, Marist Brothers, Vermont Street, St Peters College Epsom, Auckland University and Onkaparainga TAFE.

www.ingramcontent.com/pod-product-compliance
Lightning Source LLC
Chambersburg PA
CBHW031624040426
42452CB00007B/665